Critical Acclaim

Eric Koch has been explaining German culture to North America for years."
- The Globe and Mail

"It takes a great deal of imagination, background knowledge, psychological understanding and the talent of a born writer to carry it off. Mr. Koch has done so triumphantly.... Mr. Koch's amazing story, movingly and skilfully told, once again proves that the truth can be stranger than fiction, especially in dark times such as Europe during the thirties and forties."
- Walter Laqueur

"Eric Koch's brilliant, unique and moving account of two lives has the passion of personal involvement, the clarity of historical observation and the revelation of archetypal drama. It is a remarkable piece of writing."
- Adrienne Clarkson,
journalist and former
Governor-General of Canada

"His imaginative agility, inventiveness and stylish wit have enabled him to create original and highly entertaining works."
- Oxford Companion of
Canadian Literature

"Conceptually intriguing...Koch's historical novel...is intelligently written and highly informative."
- Publishers Weekly

"*The Man Who Knew Charlie Chaplin* confirms that, at its best, the historical novel brings out the importance of imagination in expanding and deepening our grasp of the past."
- *Aufbau*, New York

"...a narrative full of colourful topical detail...a spooky elegant political 'dance macabre'."
- *The Globe and Mail*

"Exciting and suspenseful..."
- *Zürichsee-Zeitungen*

"...only after the last sentence can one put this down and immediately recommend it to someone else."
- *Das Stadtmagazin Erfurt*

"...many voices...character full portraits...including humour, laconic irony...varied story-telling techniques... always new and surprising..."
- *Frankfurter Rundschau*

THE GOLDEN YEARS

**Encounters with
Glenn Gould,
Marshall McLuhan,
Lester B. Pearson,
René Lévesque
and
John G. Diefenbaker**

Five Stories

Library and Archives Canada Cataloguing in Publication

Koch, Eric, 1919-
    Encounters with Glenn Gould, Marshall McLuhan, Lester B.
Pearson, René Lévesque and John G. Diefenbaker / Eric Koch.

Also issued in electronic format.
ISBN 978-0-88962-980-6

    1. Gould, Glenn, 1932-1982. 2. McLuhan, Marshall, 1911-1980.
3. Pearson, Lester B., 1897-1972. 4. Lévesque, René, 1922-1987.
5. Diefenbaker, John G., 1895-1979. 6. Canada--Civilization--20th
century. 7. Canada--Intellectual life--20th century. I. Title.

FC25.K63 2013   971.05092'2   C2013-900859-4

Pubished by Mosaic Press, Oakville, Ontario, Canada, 2012.

MOSAIC PRESS, Publishers
Copyright © 2013 Eric Koch
ISBN 978-0-88962-980-6
eBook 978-0-88962-981-3
Designed by Eric Normann
Printed and bound in Canada.

We acknowledge the financial support of the Ontario Media Development
Corporation.

Mosaic Press in Canada: Mosaic Press in USA:
1252 Speers Road, Units 1 & 2   c/o Livingston, 40 Sonwil Dr,
Oakville, Ontario L6L 5N9   Cheektowaga, NY 14225
phone: (905) 825-2130   phone: (905) 825-2130
email: info@mosaic-press.com

www.mosaic-press.com

THE GOLDEN YEARS

**Encounters with
Glenn Gould,
Marshall McLuhan,
Lester B. Pearson,
René Lévesque
and
John G. Diefenbaker**

Five Stories

Eric Koch

mosaic press

Eric Koch

Other Books by Eric Koch

Fiction

The French Kiss
McClelland & Stewart, Toronto, 1969

The Leisure Riots
Tundra Books, Montreal, 1973
Die Freizei Revoluzzer*, Heyne Verlag, Munich

The Last Thing You'd Want to Know
Tundra Books, Montreal, 1976
Die Spanne Leben*, Heyne Verlag, Munich
(*Both German versions were reissued together
in 1987 under the title CRUPP.)

Goodnight, Little Spy
Virgo Press, Toronto, and Ram Publishing, London, 1979

Kassandrus
Heyne Verlag, Munich, 1988

Liebe und Mord auf Xananta
Verlag Eichborn, Frankfurt, 1992

Icon in Love: A Novel about Goethe
Mosaic Press, Oakville, 1998

Nobelpreis für Goethe
Fischer Tachenbuch, Frankfurt, 1999

The Man Who Knew Charlie Chaplin
Mosaic Press, Oakville, 2000

L'uomo Chi Splìo Hitler, Barbera Editoré, Siena, 2006

Earrings
Mosaic Press, Oakville, 2002

Arabian Nights 1914: A Novel about Kaiser Wilhelm II
Mosaic Press, Oakville, 2003

Premonitions
Mosaic Press, Oakville, 2008, 2009

The Weimar Triangle
Mosaic Press, Oakville, 2010

Non-fiction

Deemed Suspect
Methuen, Toronto, 1980

Inside Seven Days
Prentice-Hall, Toronto, 1986

Hilmar and Odette
McClelland & Stewart, Toronto, 1996
Chongqing Publishing House, 1998

The Brothers Hambourg
Robin Brass, Toronto, 1997

I Remember the Location Exactly
Mosaic Press, Oakville, 2007

Die Braut im Zwielicht: Erinnerungen
Weidle Verlag, Bonn, 2009

Contents

Preface

All writers of historical fiction are invariably asked: What is true? What is invented?

I made up these stories in order to tell *my* truth, to show the essence, as I saw it, of five great men who helped to shape the "sixties revolution" in Canada.

I invented the narrator. That was easy. He is a portrait of the author as a young man. But to perform the role of narrator in these stories he has only two characteristics—curiosity and ingenuity. The CBC producer I actually was in those years had one or two others that are irrelevant.

I cannot pretend I ever met Pearson or Diefenbaker personally. My encounters with the other three were so unmemorable that they do not lend themselves to storytelling.

I met Glenn Gould when he appeared in a film I produced in 1966, but we hardly spoke and we certainly did not shake hands. He was wearing gloves and I knew he did not shake hands with anybody if he could help it.

I encountered Marshall McLuhan a few times, but he always seemed to confuse me with somebody else.

I knew René Lévesque slightly when we were colleagues in Montreal in the CBC's International Service (later

Radio Canada International) in the early nineteen-fifties. I wish I still had the photo taken of me and another young broadcaster who may have been René, both waving Union Jacks, when we said goodbye to Princess Elizabeth in Newfoundland at the end of the Royal Tour in 1951. In later years I observed him only from afar. Lévesque's girlfriend, Camille, is pure fiction.

The narrator is, of course, not the only invented character in these stories. The Russian pianist and his mother are also fictitious. As far as I know, no Toronto student ever tried to explain Marshall McLuhan for money. But I made up this ploy as a device to get close to his ideas. The Pearson story is based on records of the 1958 Couchiching Conference and on Stephen Vizinczey's book *In Praise of Older Women*. I participated in the conflict on which the Diefenbaker story is based. Only the dinner party and the Texan tycoon are fiction.

The sixties revolution was a historical event. To young Canadians it is as unreal as Sir John A. Macdonald and the Riel Rebellion. To no-longer-young Canadians it was a social and cultural revolution many of them thoroughly enjoyed as their golden years.

Our five Canadians were in their prime around 1960. Glenn Gould was changing the way we make and hear music. Marshall McLuhan was teaching us to understand the media in a new way. Lester Pearson was opening the door to a new role Canada played in the world as a peace maker.

My story about René Lévesque catches him at the dramatic moment when he became a separatist.

The subject of the fifth story presents prime minister John Diefenbaker in a situation inconceivable a few years earlier. The ending is based on plausible hearsay. I believe it to be true.

For that matter, plausible hearsay is as good a description as any of both history and fiction.

Eric Koch

Glenn Gould: The Last Puritan

I T WAS NOT EVERY DAY that I received a phone call from the Soviet ambassador.

"You mentioned the other day," he opened the conversation, sounding like a bass singing Boris Godunov slightly off key, "that you know Glenn Gould. You may remember we met at the French embassy."

"Of course I remember."

In the spring of 1961 I found it useful, for a number of reasons not relevant to this story, to get myself invited to events on the diplomatic cocktail circuit in Ottawa.

"I hope you don't think it is an imposition," the ambassador continued, "if I ask for your help. A lady arrived a couple of days ago from Moscow who wishes to meet Glenn Gould. This is, in fact, the only purpose of her trip, to meet Glenn Gould. Her name is Tatyana Yaminskaya. The name may ring a bell."

"Is she by any chance related to Dmitri Yaminsky?"

"The mother."

I had a vision of the Ukrainian peasant face of Mrs. Khrushchev.

I can't carry a tune but I happen to know quite a lot about music. Dmitri Yaminsky is a superb young Soviet pianist, a couple of years younger than Glenn and often compared with him, well known for his recording of the Glazunov concerto, which is hardly ever played in the West. Glenn mentioned meeting Dmitri just before the end of his two-week tour in the USSR four years ago, in 1957—a tour, I might add, that has become a legend. It was the first time a pianist from North America performed in the USSR since the death of Stalin four years earlier. It was a magical occasion.

"Tatyana Yaminskaya," the ambassador went on, "is now on her way to Toronto, where she will be staying at the Windsor Arms Hotel. The lady would not have received permission to make this trip if she was not the widow of a senior official and was not very well connected in the highest circles."

"May I ask...?'

The ambassador did not let me finish the question. "The lady came here in a state of acute consternation. Apparently, soon after Glenn Gould's tour Dmitri had a nervous collapse. There was fear of suicide. But he recovered, with some help from the doctors, and started playing again, though not with the same energy and brilliance. But now he has had another collapse. His mother is desperate. She will grasp at any straw. One of his psychiatrists suggested a phone call from Glenn Gould, or perhaps a personal letter, might be invaluable to help him become himself again."

"I see," I said, without much enthusiasm. "This seems rather unlikely, don't you think?"

"I am not a psychiatrist," the ambassador said gruffly. "By the way, the lady used to be an English teacher. Language will not be a problem."

"Good." I tried to sound positive. "Of course I will do all I can."

"That will be a great service, also to your country. You may remember that your government was heavily involved in organizing Glenn Gould's tour in 1957."

I was grateful to the Soviet ambassador for reminding me of my obligations as a Canadian patriot.

The next day, after breakfast, I called the hotel. Tatyana Yaminskaya had arrived the evening before but was unavailable. So I left a message at the desk. After an hour she called. I suggested I visit her in the afternoon.

"I don't suppose you could come right away?"

Her English was indeed amazing.

"If you prefer."

I was immensely relieved to discover that Tatyana was the precise opposite of Mrs. Khrushchev. She had sparkling blue eyes, a wonderful complexion and a warm, winning smile, and wore an elegant dark blue dress and three rows of pearls. She looked like a movie star in a French film playing a grand duchess at the turn of the century.

Tatyana took me to the Courtyard Café, the large, tree-shaded patio in the back, where a few guests were having a late breakfast. She ordered tea.

"It is very good of you to assist me in my painful task," she said, "I appreciate it very much. No doubt you have better things to do."

I told her I was pleased to make this my priority, but Glenn was a notoriously difficult man and I was by no means sure that I could arrange a meeting. At the moment he was at his cottage on Lake Simcoe, anyway.

"Oh," she said, frowning heavily. "How terrible. The ambassador told me he was in Toronto."

"I am sorry," was all I could say.

"This is a heavy, heavy blow. I cannot stay longer than five days."

"I am quite prepared to drive you to his cottage there. But I can assure you he will not receive you."

I explained to her that Glenn is a fanatic about his privacy. He insists on being left alone with his dog. He will see nobody.

"How far is it?'

"It would take us less than three hours, depending on the traffic."

"I would not want to waste your time," she said, "unless we had his agreement to receive me beforehand. I understand my ambassador has told you why I have come. My son could be a younger brother of your friend. Also a child prodigy. A genius, everybody says. But these are words I avoid because they are so imprecise. I prefer to say that Dmitri is exceptionally gifted and exceptionally sensitive and, alas, fragile. I do not know anything about Canadian literature, but Dmitri's head is full of Dostoevsky. I hope your Canadian authors are more cheerful."

"I would think they probably are." I smiled.

"You must think that I am on—I just learned this idiom—'on a wild goose chase.' I don't blame you. You were not in Moscow and Leningrad when Glenn Gould appeared, like the first musician to land on Mars. The standards for the best piano playing in the USSR had been set by Sviatoslav Richter, Emil Gilels and Radu Lupu, and by my son. But we had never heard or seen a phenomenon like Glenn Gould, so original, so captivating, so intensely serious, so deep, so ecstatic, so *radical*. Dmitri came closest."

"You were unprepared?" I asked. "You had not heard his recording of Bach's *Goldberg Variations*?"

"No. We are less isolated than we used to be, but we still live in another world. Not only was his Bach a revelation, but the moderns on his programs were entirely new to us—people like Schönberg, who had been taboo. We had only read about them, but that was all. Especially the young people, musicians like Dmitri. For them all this was earth-shaking. My son was thrown off balance, totally. With horrible consequences. I was frightened to death. He said what was the point of struggling on, in a world that had produced Glenn Gould, in some obscure place on the other side of the planet no one had ever heard about. He would never be able to reach such heights. And then I found the draft of a suicide note on his desk…Waiter, some more tea, please."

I said nothing because there was nothing I could say. The one admittedly irreverent thought I had I could hardly reveal—namely, did I really need this? Why didn't I kill this project in the bud the moment I heard about it and tell the ambassador, "Sorry, Your Excellency, I don't think I can help. I don't know Glenn Gould well enough." Which was entirely true. Hardly anybody did. The new English idiom Tatyana had just learned—wild goose chase—seemed to me entirely appropriate to describe her mission.

"If I phone him, he won't answer," I said. "He never answers. He wants to be left alone. He may not phone me for weeks, and then only in the middle of the night, in the small hours, at two or three o'clock in the morning. And he'd keep me on the phone for an hour when all I want is to go back to sleep."

The waiter brought a new teapot.

I wanted to repeat to her what I had already told the ambassador, namely that, even if in the end we did get through to him and he complied with her request, I could not imagine anything Glenn could convey to her son that would change her son's mind. But fortunately I stopped myself. Who was I to say this? I did not know Dmitri. Obviously she thought otherwise or she would not be here.

"Do you know of anybody who visits him?" she asked. "Under the circumstances, could that not be our best approach? We might just go along and hope for the best."

"That's an excellent idea," I exclaimed. "Why didn't I think of it? It's certainly worth trying."

I pulled out my pen and scribbled on a napkin, "manager, friend(?), mother."

"You have to give me a little time," I said, getting excited. "Let me see what I can do. I will go home and do some phoning and get back to you in an hour. At the minimum, I am sure you can probably meet them. It's better than nothing. Something may occur to you while they talk that might help you."

"I don't see how. What I need is Glenn Gould himself. But I suppose you are right. One never knows."

I went to my place and phoned his agent, Hans Rosenbaum, his oldest friend Stuart Macdonald and Mrs. Gould. I told them that the mother of Dmitri Yaminisky was in town, that she was beautiful and hoped to see Glenn. She had heard him in Moscow and had little time. Were they intending to go up to Lake Simcoe during the next day or two and could they be persuaded to take her and me along? None of them said yes, but they all wanted to meet this beautiful Russian lady. Very few visitors from the Soviet Union had arrived in Toronto in recent years.

We went to see Glenn's manager, Hans Rosenbaum, first, in his basement office at home, just north of St. Clair Avenue West. Hans was in his early thirties, handsome, not tall, well groomed, just two or three years older than Glenn, who was thirty this year. They were good friends. Hans was a refugee from Nazi Germany and Glenn his first client. He had taken him on immediately after hearing his first Bach recital at the Royal Conservatory and since then struck gold.

"I've heard your son's recording of the Glazunov concerto," Hans said to Tatyana after we had taken our seats. "It is superb. I hope he'll soon be able to play in the West."

"So do I," she sighed. "Things are gradually loosening up, but Dmitri is passing through a difficult phase."

"Oh, I'm used to 'difficult phases.'" Hans laughed. "It seems you can't be a great pianist without going through a difficult phase once in a while. Just ask Horovitz's agent!"

"Perhaps you can tell us a little about Glenn's troubles, Hans," I said. "That is bound to help Mrs. Yaminskaya see her son in a new perspective."

"Glenn has serious health problems, both real and imagined. He is terrified of germs. He will not shake hands with anybody and cannot abide anybody touching him. No room is ever warm enough for him. Even at the height of summer he wears an overcoat and a woollen scarf, and at least one pair of gloves. He has to soak his hands in warm water for twenty minutes before he touches the piano. He is an insomniac. He suffers from stomach cramps, severe headaches, frequently recurring colds. He has the terrible habit of cancelling concerts at the last moment. Flying is an ordeal. Most hotels are. He cannot abide air conditioning. Surely Dmitri is not as bad as that!"

Tatyana inspected her fingernails.

"Yes—and no," she said.

Hans was not sure what she meant so he went on.

"Glenn is never satisfied unless he plays alone and nobody listens. His performances in public always leave him frustrated, dissatisfied, unhappy. He can't bear it if anybody he knows is in the concert audience. How about Dmitri? Does he behave like that?"

"Before he heard Glenn Gould," Tatyana replied, "he wasn't too bad. Moody and often depressed, yes, up and down, but it was bearable. But four years ago, after hearing Glenn Gould, he broke down and cancelled his entire season. He refused to go near the piano again. We have very good doctors. They prescribed all kinds of treatments. But he never fully recovered. That is why it was suggested that perhaps a word from Glenn Gould..."

"Hm...I see."

Clearly, Hans was at least as skeptical as I was.

"I asked you on the phone," I said to him, "whether you are intending to drive up to Lake Simcoe during the next day or two."

"I might. I will let you know."

Our next appointment was with Stuart Macdonald, the pianist's oldest friend and, during much of his childhood, his next-door neighbour. Stuart worked out of his home, only a few blocks away from Hans, and his room was crowded with books and papers. Stuart was one of Canada's leading newspaper columnists. He had a lively round face and wore glasses and seemed to be glad to be interrupted. He clearly found Tatyana attractive.

"I wish I had more time at the moment," he said. "I want to hear about musical politics in the Soviet Union and write a column about it. Maybe tomorrow or the next day?"

Tatyana said she would be delighted. Maybe they could talk about it in the car on the way to Glenn's *dacha?*

"Maybe," he laughed. "But I have three deadlines at the moment. Now, what would you like to know about Glenn that you don't already know? After all, he talks about himself incessantly, with brilliant verbosity, in print, on the radio, on television; he enjoys giving abstruse interviews, has breath-taking self-confidence that often makes him talk about things he knows little about, uses big words and long sentences that sometimes sound as though they were translated from boring German textbooks and loves clowning around and mimicking people, which he does amazingly well. You also probably know that he reads a lot, that he calls himself *The Last Puritan,* identifying himself with the hero of George Santayana's story about self-education, that he loves Russian novels and Thomas Mann, that he wants to compose and conduct, is in touch with all the latest recording technologies, is deeply superstitious and talks freely about his dreams, is pathologically picky about his pianos, insists on sitting on a low folding chair when he plays, which he usually carries with him—what else?—oh yes, that he says he loves animals more than human beings, that he often makes friends with people and then drops them for no apparent reason, which is very upsetting to them, that he is very interested in the stock market and keeps on top of the day's political news and tells the entire world at great length what music he likes and does not like, and why, especially if he can shock people by saying that the trouble with Mozart was that he lived too long."

"Does he say that?" Tatyana smiled.

"Yes, he also believes Mozart didn't know how to write a piano concerto. He says he doesn't care much for music written between Bach's *Art of the Fugue* and *Tristan,* which then leads to his favourites, Hindemith and Schönberg, Alban Berg and Webern. With the exception of some Haydn, some Beethoven—but not what he calls the heroic and pompous Beethoven of the middle period—a lot of Mendelssohn, strangely enough, and Richard Strauss whom he admired *hugely.* But that's not what you want to know."

"No. I want to know how he pulls himself together after he has been sick."

"By taking pills. He keeps our entire pharmaceutical industry happy single-handedly. You cannot imagine how many pills he takes. For every occasion. He consults doctors all the time, makes them prescribe pills of every colour and doesn't listen to them. He tells *them* what is wrong with him."

"I see. What about girlfriends?"

"He is secretive about them. Nobody knows for sure and I wouldn't ask. I know he receives a lot of love letters from girls he has not met. I don't know what he does with them. He likes to gossip about other people's sex lives but about his own he is very puritanical."

Tatyana frowned.

"Did you say puritanical?"

"Yes," Stuart Macdonald laughed, "the Toronto Presbyterian kind, not the Soviet or Russian-Orthodox-Ascetic kind."

"I'm not sure I follow you."

"I mean other teenagers of Glenn's background rebelled against their parents' Presbyterian horror of sensual pleasures. Which was typical of the Toronto of Glenn's childhood. When Glenn was thirteen and fourteen, he saw nothing incompatible between his parents' Puritanism and his overwhelming urge to make and understand music. He never rebelled. There was no need. I did, but he did not. That puritanical tradition shaped his musical tastes. Not right away, but eventually. That is why he dislikes what he thinks of as sensual, self-indulgent, emotional music and prefers rational, abstract, well-structured, cerebral, otherworldly music. He says he believes in Bach's God and is not interested in music that does not meet his ethical and spiritual standards. When he was a boy he never used four-letter words, unlike the other boys, me included."

"What kind of words?" Tatyana wondered, turning to me.

While I tried to explain to her what a four-letter word was—not easy for a gentleman like me—the telephone rang, reminding Stuart Macdonald of one of his three deadlines. So we took our leave.

The next morning I picked up Tatyana and drove out to the comfortable neighbourhood of the Beaches in the east end of the city, to 32 Southwood Drive, the Gould home, to visit Glenn's mother, Florence, whom I never found particularly appealing and who was certainly, compared to Tatyana, decidedly unspectacular. I always found her husband, Bert, more agreeable, but he was dominated by his wife and Glenn, and never quite understood why Nature had given him and his wife such an extraordinary son who never had the slightest inclination to follow him in the fur business.

I repeated to Florence what I had said on the telephone. Was she going to visit Glenn during the next few days?

"I really had no intention," she said. "I talk to Glenn almost every evening and try to leave him alone. But, of course, if I can be useful, I would like to help. One musician's mother," she smiled, "must help another musician's mother." I noted that she carefully avoided saying "one *genius's* mother," etc.) "It would depend very much on what Glenn would have to say. I will ask him tonight."

She did and, to my great surprise, Glenn said Dmitri Yaminsky's mother and I were more than welcome, as long as we didn't stay longer than two hours *at the most.*

We drove up the following day. In the car, Florence and Tatyana compared notes. Both mothers had made enormous efforts to make sure their sons had normal childhoods. Neither mother was particularly successful. Their sons' talents set them apart and isolated them. Florence was a piano teacher and taught Glenn herself until he was ten. Both boys detested school and wanted to become professional pianists when they were five. Both strongly disliked competitive sports. Both had remarkable musical memories at an early age. Glenn had memorized all of Bach's preludes and fugues in the first book of the "Forty-eight" by the time he was ten. When Dmitri was ten, he knew the first ten Beethoven sonatas and all seven Scriabin sonatas by heart.

Glenn's black-and-white shaggy sheepdog, Banquo, greeted us enthusiastically when we arrived. Glenn welcomed Tatyana with great warmth and charm. It was a lovely, sunny spring day. The *dacha*, the lake, the landscape generally, she said, reminded her very much of her place near Moscow.

He seated the four of us on deckchairs on the lawn looking out at the lake. "Mother told me you are worried about Dmitri," he said to Tatyana after we had settled down.

"Yes." She made a determined effort not to waste time and to come straight to the point. "He has again cancelled all his concerts."

"Again?" Glenn rubbed his chin.

"Yes, he did it the first time after hearing you play."

"Surely you don't believe that?"

"Oh yes. No question about it."

"Let me assure you, *madame,* that was only an excuse. I know how these things work. When you are about to explode, you'll think of any reason. I cancel concerts when I have a little twitch in my left toe, never mind how many people I upset and how much money I lose. Dmitri's timing was a mere coincidence."

Tatyana explained the course of events and said that the connection with him, Glenn, was not only Dmitri's own opinion and also the view of a number of doctors they had consulted. It was one of them who had suggested a word from him, Glenn, might make all the difference.

Florence felt she had to come out on Tatyana's side.

"Surely you can think of something constructive to say, Glenn," she said. "Obviously you made a great impression on him."

Glenn turned to me with a twinkle.

"What do you think I should say to Dmitri Yaminsky?"

"I think you should say what Schopenhauer would say."

"No," Glenn beamed. "I will say what the old Tolstoy would say. 'What took you so long to see the light?' he would say. 'Concert audiences are forces of evil. Get rid of them! They bring about mob rule. Slavery. They are enemies of Truth and Beauty, instruments of the devil. Tell the devil to go to hell where he belongs! Become a free man at last! Throw away the shackles. Become yourself!'"

Tatyana stared at him.

"Concert audiences?" she gasped. "How can Dmitri do without them?"

"Make recordings! Edit the tapes until you are satisfied. Throw out the mistakes. Come as close to perfection as it is possible for a mere mortal. Take your time! Relax! Live up to your own standards and be faithful to what you believe the composer had in mind. Don't believe the sordid propaganda that says a performer must communicate with a live audience to be at his best. That is a dastardly lie perpetrated by concert managers and people who go to concerts not to hear music but to torture performers, to take sadistic delight in the false notes they play, show off their clothes and pick up the latest gossip in the intermission. After all, people used to love going to executions, too!"

• • •

As the whole world knows, Dmitri Yaminsky followed Glenn's advice. His latest recording of the *Goldberg Variations* is outselling Glenn's two to one.

Understanding Marshall

EVERY MONDAY EVENING Marshall McLuhan conducted a seminar at the Centre for Culture and Technology, a coach house on St. Joseph Street hidden behind other buildings, just south of St. Michael's College at the University of Toronto. The doors were open to one and all. By the fall of 1966 McLuhan was a world celebrity. There was often standing room only for the latecomers among the scholars, students, artists, advertising people, politicians and lay visitors who attended. Many people, especially academics, were, to put it mildly, unconvinced by his main insight, that the course of history was determined, to a considerable extent, by the methods of communication available and by the way we received information, and that at the present stage, these methods of communication were passing from the print era to the electric era. Our perceptions were, therefore, changing in a fundamental way, with profound and surprising consequences for the way we live. Many people considered his explorations, probes he called them, impenetrable and were upset and sometimes hostile.

However, few denied that his charm and wit, his aphorisms and paradoxes, his playfulness generally, were great entertainment, and so was his talent for playing verbal games with his audience "putting it on," was the phrase used to describe it. Only rarely did a skeptic upset him. Many of the participants had read at least parts of his recent book, *Understanding Media*, i.e., understanding him, Marshall McLuhan. But they still didn't. He had turned his back on the traditional ways of explaining things and usually declined to provide evidence for the many unexpected observations he made. To do so would be "linear," he explained, a leftover from the print age, and therefore inherently unsuited to throwing light on the new electric world of television and computers.

I saw no reason why I should not cash in on his fame by trying to bridge the chasm between him and the thousands who wanted to understand him but could not. So one Monday evening, after everybody else had gone home, I accompanied him to the parking lot. As usual, he was wearing a Harris tweed suit and was well groomed, handsome, bright-eyed and generally in good shape for a man of fifty-four.

"Marshall," I said, "I am hatching a plot and I need your help."

"I'll do anything as long as it doesn't cost me a single coffee spoon."

"A coffee spoon?"

"Don't you know *The Love Song of J. Alfred Prufrock*? 'I have measured out my life with coffee spoons.'"

"Oh, I see. I'm sorry I have never read it. But I see what you mean. This will actually save you time. My plan will keep blockheads off your back. I want to rent a place somewhere near the campus and start a little business explaining you to the world. I will put an ad in the *Toronto Star* and see what happens. Assuming that you will give me your blessing, would you please recommend a couple of former graduate students of yours who need money? I will charge the customers forty dollars for thirty minutes' consultation. Your two students can keep twenty. And I will keep twenty. Your reward would be the deep satisfaction that you have done a good deed for two of your starving disciples."

"And for you, who, from the look of things, has more than enough to eat."

This remark was not entirely fair. For a man of thirty-six I had so far avoided a middle-aged spread. But I decided to let it go.

'Yes, thank you, I do, Marshall."

"All right. You have my blessing. I will call you in the morning with two names. I must get their consent first. I will also check it out with my agent. But I am sure she won't object."

Always prompt and reliable, he called me around eleven o'clock.

"I have two names for you. As you requested. They both know my work well. One is Elizabeth Huntley, now an underemployed actress. She is lively and good-looking and has already been married twice, once to a trumpeter, and once to a Platonist. Which is more than anybody can say about you, as far as I know. Some male customers may wish to stay for a full hour. Don't worry, I won't expect any extra reward for my role as pimp. And the other person is a man who has just spent six months in a mental institution. Probably he just suffered from depression, nothing terrible. I saw him last week. He strikes me as perfectly normal. His name is Richard Long. He told me an amazing story. While he was there, a group of ordinary people volunteered to pretend to be mad. They easily got themselves admitted. The doctors who treated them were unable to detect that they were so-called 'sane.' However, the patients noticed it immediately. They could see that they were *playing*. This goes to show that the ability to play, the good humour needed to enter into fun and games, is the final mark of sanity."

"That is why you are such a sane man," I said. "Well, thank you, Marshall. I will keep you informed."

I had no trouble at all renting two large rooms on the ground floor of a house close to the campus, on the southeast corner of Willcocks and Huron, with a balcony facing Huron Street, available immediately. The grey-haired, kind-hearted landlady was Finnish. I explained to her what I was doing, that one of the rooms was to be a waiting room, the other a consulting room, and that I hoped there would be a constant flow of people coming and going. I said I would make sure she would not have to open the door when visitors rang. I would do it. She accepted this arrangement cheerfully and pointed out that visitors could also use the balcony as an additional entrance and exit, which was certainly an added advantage.

Before putting an ad in the paper, I met both candidates. Marshall could not have done better. Elizabeth Huntley was in her mid twenties and looked like a robust Judy Garland. Richard Long was a little older, with steel-rimmed glasses and a pony tail. He seemed to spent his nights in the coffee houses of Yorkville, on borrowed money, probably smoking pot and who knows what else. Both said Marshall had changed their lives. I explained that we would have to work out a timetable, to divide up the chores between them. I made it clear that I often intended to be present since I was also anxious to learn.

I received twenty-seven answers to this ad:

Stop Being A Global Village Idiot!
Take Lessons in Understanding
Marshall McLuhan.
One 30-minute Questioning of a
McLuhan Student – $40

Our first client was an elderly Ukrainian sales clerk in a supermarket on Dufferin Street.

"What's all this about a global village?" he asked Elizabeth Huntley. They were sitting opposite each other on easy chairs, near the Huron Street balcony. I had made myself comfortable on a sofa.

"It's really quite simple." Elizabeth was wearing a dark green sweater and a black skirt, a deliberately unglamorous costume to prevent any unnecessary digressions. "We are now living in an era when information is communicated with the speed of light. This has made it possible for the whole world to live in one village, the global village. We call our present time the electric era, or, if you prefer, the electronic era. The preceding era was the print era, which began about five hundred years ago. It took the place of illiterate tribalism when communications were conducted largely by word of mouth. Our current electric period is more like the tribal era than the print era."

"Do you mean we're all going back to the jungle?" the client asked.

"That is not the language we use. We watch patterns and ask questions. In fact, we enjoy asking questions far more than we enjoy providing answers. We do a lot of guessing and speculating. Our one big insight is that a lot of the things that are happening in the world are connected to the way we communicate with one another. For most of us, this is hard to grasp because it's a new idea. It's also a new way of looking at the past. One particular insight is that print led to individualism and to a linear way of thinking, called linear because we read a book line by line. And we're alone when we read. Hence the individualism. And we read with our eyes, which makes it possible that we can easily verify things. Hence the rationalism. This does not mean that people were actually more reasonable than they had been before or have been since. Far from it.

"I'm still living in what you call the print era," the client said, scratching the back of his head.

"Of course." Elizabeth smiled. "We all do, to a large extent. The various periods overlap. In any case, many of these changes in perception are subliminal."

"What does that mean?"

"We are not aware of them. For example, we are not aware of the shift of emphasis from the eye to ear, from visual space to acoustic space."

"Now you've lost me."

"I don't blame you," Elizabeth assured him. "I was lost the first time I heard this as well. I simply could not believe that in the new electric era, when we live in acoustic space with centres everywhere and boundaries nowhere, we can in a sense—so I was told—hear everything simultaneously that happens on the planet Earth since information travels with the speed of light. There's a renewed emphasis on the community, on the tribe, big and small. Unlike our eyes, which focus, our ears favour collectivity. They are not focused. Acoustic space enhances inner experience. The Greek poet Homer was blind. He didn't need any eyes. He couldn't write, anyway. He was illiterate. He didn't mind being illiterate since he had never heard of writing. He spoke his verses and others remembered them and eventually wrote them down."

"Now let's come down to Earth," the client, drumming his fingers irritably on the arm of his easy chair. "Forget about Homer. How can you actually tell that people today are more collectivity-minded than they used to be?"

"One way of telling is that young people are suddenly looking for their communal roots. Their parents were less interested. If you have children or grandchildren they've probably asked you all kinds of questions about the past. Am I right?"

"Yes, you're right." He brightened up considerably. "My grandchildren keep asking questions my children never asked. The place where my great grandfather was born, and that sort of thing. And most of them I can't answer."

"And look at the way various groups are getting together and demanding an end to discrimination," Elizabeth continued. "Blacks and French Canadians, and many others. It's a new tribalism. People are more and more proud of the tribe they belong to. Of course they don't use the word."

"I can see that."

He needed a little pause to absorb all this.

"There's one thing you said," he resumed, "that worries me. I don't think there's anything better than reason. Which you say is now passé, since it belonged to the print era. I mean, I am a religious man but I still think that in everyday affairs there's no substitute for reason, for being rational. Are we going to be governed by a bunch of madmen who just follow their instincts?"

"Not at all," Elizabeth assured him. "I just said belief in reason did not make people more reasonable. In the French Revolution people cut off a lot of heads in the name of reason. Since today, in the electric age, ordinary people can communicate instantaneously in a way they never could before, they can participate in the running of things much more easily than they ever used to. Ordinary people are not mad."

"Well, that's encouraging."

Elizabeth looked at her watch.

"I just said I am a religious man. What do you think about the future of religion?"

"We don't make predictions. But we look at patterns, as I said. Let me get at your question in a roundabout way. This will tie together some of the ideas we have been talking about. Take the business of looking for roots. A person who looks for roots has no body. Don't take this literally—this is kind of poetic, I know. In the electric age you have no body. You use the telephone: all there is of you is your voice. You stand in front of a television camera: all there is of you is your picture. You have no body. And when you have no body you look for your origins, for your identity. The word we use is 'discarnate.' The new reality in the electric age is that of 'discarnate man.' Man without a natural body."

"If you say so." He frowned. "But what has it to do with religion?"

"Isn't it obvious? When you are nobody, when you don't have a natural body; the void must be filled with the spiritual."

For the first time during the entire conversation, the client smiled.

"So you think religion is going to make a comeback?"

"To the extent that religion is a response to our spiritual needs, yes. I have no doubt. On the other hand, many people will take drugs. They already do. There probably will be all kinds of new religions, and new cults. But, I repeat, I must be careful. We make no predictions. We only look around us and observe."

The client happily paid us our money and went home.

My business was booming. Our clients were usually satisfied and recommended us to their friends. I felt like an eye doctor's nurse who had to make appointments weeks in advance. But I procrastinated about asking Marshall for another poor student and renting more space. I did not wish to be in this business forever, however profitable and beneficial. And I preferred listening to Marshall himself, undistilled, on Monday evenings, to hearing his views second hand from his two disciples, covering the same ground again and again. Both did very well. Only one of Elizabeth's clients, a swashbuckling garage mechanic, made a nuisance of himself and refused to leave the premises unless she agreed to have dinner with him. She had to ask me to help her dispose of him through the balcony, which seemed to amuse him more than it did us.

A number of our clients challenged everything they were told. They usually enjoyed the sessions but at the end of the half-hour they were just as skeptical as they were at the beginning. One of these was the formidable, aggressive, English-born Catherine McBurney, a retired high school teacher who looked like a younger sister of the actress Margaret Rutherford and had the same double chin. She constantly interrupted Richard Long's exercise in advanced McLuhanism. I was reminded of Marshall's definition of an argument: it is when two people are trying to have the last word at the same time.

Catherine:

Now, what's all this about the medium being the message? Does this mean that when I read a newspaper it doesn't matter what's in it—all that matters is that I am reading a newspaper? Isn't your clever-clever friend profoundly mischievous when he says content does not matter?

Richard:

No. He says nothing of the kind. *The medium is the message* is a paradox that contains many ideas. Let us just say that it says that the technology in which we receive information has a bearing on the information we receive, but, in a sense, it has also become part of it.

Catherine:

Do I have to take your word for this?

Richard:

All you have to do is think about it. When you read a novel, you have one kind of experience. When you see the same story told to you by word of mouth, it is another kind of experience. When you see it on the screen, it's something else again. When you receive it translated into the language of computers, you are encountering a substantially different animal.

Catherine:

That's pretty obvious. So why are you making such a fuss about it?

Richard:

Because every technology creates its own environment. When the message gets to us by electric circuitry, we get far more information than we ever got before. The world has to find new ways of coping with this. There is a need for recognizing new patterns. In the compressed high-speed systems in which we live, these patterns are often mythic.

Catherine:
Mythic? As in Greek mythology? I haven't noticed that. You mean primitive?

Richard:
We are not afraid of that word. We don't use it in a pejorative sense.

Catherine:
Make up your mind! Are we going forward or backward?

Richard:
We think the play of circuitry, of instant feedback, demands a great increase in human autonomy and human awareness. In the print era, there was a split between the head and the heart. In the electric era this split will be healed.

Catherine:
You hope.

Richard:
Yes, we hope.

Catherine:
What about violence? Will we have more of it? Less of it?

Richard:
When people have been robbed of their identity they become violent. That's the way they find out who they are. They have to discover where their boundaries are, what kind of people they are confronting. So, to answer your question whether we will have more or less violence depends on the way we cope with groups who are looking for their identity and can't find it in non-violent ways.

Catherine:
You mean, we only have wars because some people are looking for their so-called identities? I'll never believe that!

Did the Germans unleash two world wars because they were trying to find out who they were?
Richard:
Yes.
Richard ducked as she tried to hit him with her umbrella.

• • •

The following Monday evening a biology student named Tania Knox attended Marshall's seminar. She was one of the first to arrive and parked in his spot. He found another spot but left a note on her windscreen. *I would be grateful if in future you did not park in my spot. Signed, Marshall M.*
She left before him and saw the message.
She wrote a reply and put it on his windscreen.
Dear Professor McLuhan,
I apologize. Your note was the first writing of yours I understood. Signed, Tania Knox.

Lester Pearson: Love and Politics at Lake Couchiching

E VERY AUGUST I LISTENED to the Couchiching Conference for one week, from eight to nine in the evening
on the CBC radio network. I knew that the talks, debates
and discussions on public questions, national and international, conducted at the YMCA's Geneva Park, were an
annual ritual for the radio audience, which included many
politicians in Ottawa, and for the three hundred ordinary
people who attended, paying eighty dollars a person for the
week's room, board and the pleasures of consorting with
each other and with celebrity thinkers. But I had always
been averse to going myself. I knew that Geneva Park was a
singularly beautiful spot on the banks of Lake Couchiching
eighty miles north of Toronto, but if I wanted to breathe
the purifying air of the Canadian north I preferred to do
it in silence. I felt no urge to participate.

But this time, the summer of 1958, when the subject
was CRISIS '58, I overcame my scruples and went.

The speaker who delivered the keynote address in Copeland
Hall on Saturday, August 9, which opened the week's
conference, was a former history professor at the Univer-
sity of Toronto, Lester B. Pearson, now the Leader of the
Opposition. As Canada's Secretary of State for External
Affairs, and as President of the United Nations General

Assembly in 1952–53, he had played a major role in dozens of international crises culminating in the Suez affair last October, a role for which he received the Nobel Peace Prize in December.

It so happens that—by pure chance—I was present when he received the news about his Nobel Prize. To set the scene I would like to relate how this came about.

Some time ago I told my friend Larry Reynolds, an old student of Pearson's with whom he kept in touch, that I was interested in politics. So he took me along to see him a few times in Ottawa. In those days, before the government fell, Pearson was still Secretary of State for External Affairs. I was, of course, quite intimidated at first, not being used to meeting famous men. But he soon put me at ease, and so did Larry, who was clearly used to discussing big subjects with him and was quite relaxed. Before they started I had a surprise. Pearson asked Larry—of all things—what was happening on the baseball front.

Larry was prepared.

"Yesterday the Chicago White Sox beat the Yankees eight to four."

"Oh, that's too bad," Pearson said. "That was the second loss in a row. My friends in New York must be very unhappy. Now go ahead, Larry. What is on your mind?"

I noticed that he had a slight lisp.

"I wanted to pick up from what you said last time we met," Larry responded. "Surely the problem is that high ideals won't stop people from becoming aggressive from time to time."

"That's nonsense. I never said anything of the sort," Pearson spoke with unexpected heat. "We live in our own national societies without war or chaos. So it must be in the international society. No, I don't think at all it's a question of becoming aggressive from time to time. I think the situation is more interesting. Most of us are aggressive *all the time* but have been conditioned to control our in-born aggressiveness in the interest of living together. We have learned, often the hard way, to compromise with each other and become tolerant because experience has taught us that there is no alternative if we want to live decent, civilized lives. That strikes me as pretty obvious. But what is not quite so obvious is why, once in a while, normally peaceful, civilized men and women become savage animals under the incitements of collective emotion. Can you answer that?"

"I can't," Larry said, because he couldn't.

"Let me tell you a story about our true nature," Pearson continued. He removed a strand of hair from his forehead in a characteristically boyish gesture. It was hard to believe that he was over sixty. "In 1940, on Christmas eve in London the air-raid sirens began to wail. Before the wail ended I heard the bursts of the anti-aircraft guns, and between those bursts the deeper, menacing sound of bombs. It wasn't a big raid but one or two of the bombs fell a little too close to my room for my liking. I was reading in bed. To drown out the sound I turned on the radio. I was fumbling aimlessly with the dial when the room was flooded with the beauty and peace of Christmas carols. Glorious waves of the music wiped out the sound of war and conjured up visions of peaceful pre-war Christmases I remembered. Then I heard the announcer's voice. *He spoke German!* I was listening to a German station and they were Germans who were singing those carols, with their message of peace and salvation."

I was moved by this story because he was. And so was Larry.

It was a few months later, last October, after the government had fallen, that I witnessed the historic scene when he got the news of the Nobel Prize. Once again Larry had taken me along to see him.

Pearson was talking about Mackenzie King.

"King wanted to appear to be meek and passive," he said. "But you could never predict what he was going to do. He always picked the brightest people he could find to put in his cabinet and always listened to them. They often had very different temperaments from his. I have no idea what he would have said about my efforts at the time to bring about the formation of a United Nations emergency force, which ended the Suez Crisis. In private he was often fed up with the British and had strong emotional ties to the Americans. He may well have approved of my efforts to convince the British that the world had changed, that their empire had become an anachronism, that the power had shifted from London to Washington and that they had better learn to behave accordingly. Maybe it was the secret of his success that nobody could ever be sure of what he thought."

At that moment the telephone rang.

"Did you say the Canadian Press?" Pearson asked.

The answer seemed to be yes.

"What do you mean...whether I have any statement to make. About what?"

There was a pause.

"Oh, you only say this to make me feel good. A lot of people are nominated every year."

There was another pause.

"You mean I was awarded the Nobel Peace Prize? And you have the text of the telegram in front of you?"

The Canadian Press man read it to him.

All Pearson could say before Larry and I congratulated him was—

"Gosh!"

• • •

Now back to his keynote address at the Couchiching Conference half a year later. His focus was the confrontation between the USA "and no one else" and the power of the USSR, which was now "nuclear, stratospheric and supersonic." This would be serious enough if the relationship was reasonably friendly instead of very unfriendly. At the end of his speech he said it was time we began to think anew and act anew to rise to the challenge of the new occasion.

"If we don't," he concluded, "we will be fortunate if next year at Couchiching we are in a position to discuss anything at all."

During the question-and-answer period a handsome young man, probably a student, wearing a black turtleneck sweater and looking like an exotic Lord Byron, went to the microphone and asked a question in a strange foreign accent. The moderator, the barrister J.S. Midanik, had to ask him to repeat it.

"My name is András Mezei," the young man said. "I am one of a quarter million refugees from Hungary who left because the Soviets marched in while you, sir, were dealing with the Suez Canal. Please, sir, why did you not mention the Hungarian crisis in your address?"

"Oh," Mr. Pearson replied with his slight lisp, shaking his youthful lock of hair from his middle-aged forehead, "I do apologize. I certainly should have mentioned it. The speaker is quite right to point out, at least by implication, that we should have acted more vigorously to counter the brutal Soviet repression in Hungary. We did consider various steps but could not come to a decision. He is quite right. We were too preoccupied with the events in the Middle East. And of course everyone was terrified that one false step might lead to World War Three. I am grateful to him for raising this painful subject."

After the session, I stood by as the young Hungarian talked to a number of young girls in very short skirts. I could not hear what he said to them in his strong accent—he had to repeat it twice—but it was not hard to figure it out from the way the girls said no.

"Too bad," he shrugged cheerfully and went home across the parking lot to the students' barracks. I learned later that young girls left him cold and that he was not a student at all but a recently hired lecturer in European studies at the University of Saskatchewan. He had been sent all the way to Couchiching by the imaginative dean to become acquainted "with the way educated Canadians think."

The next morning I made a point of introducing myself to András Mezei at one of the breakfast tables, but of course did not mention the little exchange with the girls. We had been served at the buffet with lumpy porridge, semi–hard-boiled eggs, greasy bacon and moist toast. The YMCA had many virtues but preparing edible food was not one of them. The topic for the evening's discussion was "Disengagement: Solution in Europe?" and the speakers were Fritz Erler, Deputy Floor Leader of the Social Democratic Party in Bonn, and Robert Bowie, former Assistant Secretary of State and now the Director of International Affairs at Harvard. Putting a European versus an American with a Canadian moderator in the middle was a specialty of the Couchiching Conference planners. On this occasion the moderator was the Canadian journalist-academic Robert McKenzie, on the faculty of the London School of Economics and Political Science.

Fritz Erler sat at our table. The others were two pleasant-looking lady-librarians from Windsor, Ontario, and a silver-haired economist from Ottawa. András had heard that Erler had been incarcerated in various penitentiaries during the war, but he knew none of the details and asked him about it.

"It saved my life," Erler said. He had an oval face, wore horn-rimmed glasses and spoke remarkably good English. "I was convicted in 1939 for preparing high treason. Only preparing it, that was all. I was lucky. Had they considered my crime actual high treason I would have been executed right away. I was also lucky that I was not sent to a concentration camp. There my chances of survival would have been minimal. I only spent a short period in two small camps, the rest in a penitentiary. My one great adventure was escaping from a prisoners' transport in April 1945. I just jumped out of the truck and nobody noticed."

András was fascinated.

"Oh, I know about those army trucks," he said. "I was on many of them myself. But mine were American."

"How is that possible?" Erler asked. "How old were you at the end of the war?

"Twelve," András answered. "Nearly thirteen. We were refugees in Salzburg. I had been to a Hungarian cadet school—it was horrible—and suddenly I found myself in an American camp, with lots and lots to eat, making myself useful to the Americans in many, many interesting ways. And got paid for it. Using those trucks."

"In what interesting ways?" one of the pleasant librarians asked.

"I found women for the American soldiers. Only a few of the women were prostitutes. The one I liked best was a beautiful and elegant countess who had a castle and a count and four little countesses to feed. The women were rewarded with food and cigarettes, and often with some nice things from the PX stores."

"Tell us again—how old did you say you were, twelve?" the pleasant librarian asked. "And did you know what all this was about?"

"What do you mean?" Andreas asked indignantly. "I was not five, I was twelve! Do you mean did I sleep with the countess myself? The answer is no. Though I was old enough to want to. And I was certainly capable of it."

"You *were?*"

"Yes, I was. But I was too shy to ask."

Fritz Erler thought it was wise to change the subject.

"It must be very hard for people on this side of the ocean," he said, putting his hand on András's sleeve, "to imagine what things were like in Europe at the end of the war. I hope to talk about this tonight. And perhaps you can come up with another nice question," he added with a smile.

"I will try to think of something."

Neither András nor I attended the church service in Copeland Hall at eleven. Instead, the two of us went for a walk, along the cottages, past the tennis courts where we sat down on a bench, next to a couple of teenage boys with rackets in their hands waiting to play themselves, to watch a game between Gordon Hawkins, the associate director of the Canadian Association for Adult Education, and an attractive woman, a blooming blond lavender beauty who reminded me of the ads for Yardley soap. I had noticed her last evening and hoped to find a way to encounter her soon. She was probably around thirty-five.

"Now, András, there's a woman I would like to meet," I said.

"That's my mum." One of the boys had overheard me. "I'll introduce you, if you like."

"Oh, please."

A few minutes later the game was over. The lady had beaten Gordon Hawkins six to four and was in high spirits. The boy duly introduced his mother.

"Oh, what a pleasure it is to meet you," she said to me. Then she turned to András. "I admired your courage in asking Pearson that question last night."

"Courage? I did not need any courage for that," András replied. "I need courage to ask you to go to the beach with me this afternoon."

The lady burst into laughter.

"Do I need courage to say I would be delighted?"

"You are very charming, *madame*," András smiled.

"And you are very..."—she was looking for the right word—"foreign."

I knew in the game of love András would beat me six to one.

András and I continued our walk.

"I suppose this lady is not used to being invited to go to the beach with a young man she does not know," he said.

"After all, at the beach one is nearly naked. She would be quite accustomed to be invited by a stranger to a drink of 'rye and ginger' in any of the rooms. But not to go with him to the beach. Is that not true?"

"Probably."

"I was warned about this by the taxi driver who drove me to town when I arrived at the airport in April. He turned out to be a nice fat Austrian who gave me a useful lecture about Canadians. He said Canadians love money first, which he thought was perfectly alright. Then comes liquor, then TV, then food. Sex is way down the list. At home it is at the top of the list where it belongs. Where is it on your list?"

"I think it is somewhere in the middle." I was pleased to be asked about a subject close to my heart. "But we Canadians will soon catch up. We are still very puritanical."

"So I have learned," he said. "My taxi driver was right. Here they drink instead of having sex. In Canada puritans are drunkards, not lovers. Even here, at the YMCA."

"*Especially* here at the YMCA," I laughed. "The YMCA does not allow drinking in public, you see. That is why everybody brings a bottle, to be consumed in private in their rooms. But wait. The week is still young—it's only Sunday. People have to get to know one another before they jump into bed."

"Why?" Andreas opened his eyes wide. "I don't understand that at all. At home they first sleep together and then, if they have had fun, *then* they become acquainted."

"Why don't you try that out on this nice lady at the beach this afternoon?"

I was rightly known for giving my friends constructive advice in times of need.

"I certainly will. Since she thinks I am so foreign," he replied thoughtfully, "she probably expects it."

I did not have a chance to speak to András again until after the evening session. In the meantime I had found out that the name of the lavender beauty was Ann and that her husband was a reporter for one of the Toronto papers.

András and I sat together as we listened to Fritz Erler paint a grim picture of the tense situation in Europe. Erler wondered what would happen if, once West Germany had tactical nuclear weapons, the oppressed population in Soviet-occupied Germany would rise again, as it had in June 1953 and as the Hungarians had last October. He warned that continuing the atomic arms race and maintaining the explosive status quo in Europe were no substitute for a constructive policy of disengagement.

Robert Bowie, however, did not think the time for disengagement had as yet come. If both sides were merely concerned with security, no doubt some sort of accommodation could be worked out. But, as far as he could see, the Soviet empire had only one fundamental purpose, and that was to expand its control. Between that purpose and western interests, there was no common ground for genuine negotiation.

At the short non-alcoholic reception following the session, I reminded András that he had told Erler he would think of something to ask him. I said I was disappointed that he had not done so.

"Oh, I could not concentrate," he replied. "I kept thinking of Ann. I have decided I don't really want her. Even though she is just the right age for me. Older women know what's important and what isn't. I don't like young girls."

"You mean," I smiled, "you don't want to tell me that she rejected you."

"No, not at all. She did not reject me. Not at first, anyway. I was quite surprised, considering that she is Canadian. Of course we only talked. I did not touch her. Even though we were lying quite close to each other, on the grass, a little out of the way, almost naked, and there was nobody in sight. Her two boys were out on their bicycles. I think she wanted me to kiss her. Nobody would have noticed. I did not."

"Why not?" I asked.

"Because she had already turned me down. What would have been the point? We would have got all excited for nothing. I did what you suggested. I asked her politely if we could be together tomorrow afternoon while her husband was taking notes at one of the discussion groups. She said no."

"Naturally," I observed. "This is not Hungary."

"I know, I know," he said sadly. "But she already told me that she liked me and that she didn't love her husband."

"She told you that?"

"Not exactly. She said she only loved him in a way. I think that meant she would welcome a change. But she also said she had never slept with anyone else."

"And what did you say to that?'

"I said God forbid that I spoil a good marriage." She was quite upset when I said that. "She said that's not the way you're supposed to talk. You're suppose to seduce me." So I told her I was sorry I was such a disappointment to her.

"This is getting a little too complicated for me," I said. "What did you call us Canadians? Puritanical? Because she would not cheat on her husband but still wanted you to kiss her?"

"I suppose so. Well, anyway," András declared firmly, "I have made up my mind. I don't need her."

Three days passed. Both András and I skipped the Monday session on "The USA and the World Economy." On Tuesday evening the subject was "Science and Survival." András left during the coffee break. The main speaker, Ellis Johnson, Director of Operations at John Hopkins Research Office, who had been technical director in the U.S. Air Force Office of Atomic Energy, contended that, "God willing, there will be no physical problem of man that would not yield to the knowledge and application of science for at least two centuries." This struck me as somewhat overconfident. But nobody challenged him on that score. There was not a word in the question-and-answer period about non-physical problems. Nor was there any suggestion that in the years to come science might come under a cloud for having brought about the nuclear age and for contributing so much to the arms race. Other disciplines would touch on non-physical problems, above all on the only question young people were interested in. They wanted to know about the purpose, if any, of our existence. What did scientists have to say about that? Nothing!

On Wednesday evening there was another session about the Cold War, asking what strategies the West should pursue. In this session Fritz Erler spoke once again. But I learned far more on Thursday evening, even though the title "Propaganda and the Uncommitted Nations" struck me as not particularly promising. I wondered why András missed it. Was he having better luck with another older woman? He had already mentioned to me that he found more and more couples, men and women not married to each other, holding hands during the discussions. How did he know they were not married, I asked? Because married people don't hold hands *anywhere,* he explained to me. He said he had also noticed that there was a distinct change of atmosphere, a general loosening of the tone, less formality altogether, a considerable improvement in fact. He had even seen a couple embracing in a boat, way out on the lake, before dinner, during the drinking hour. Could one of them have been Murray Ross, the Vice-President of the University of Toronto and President of the Canadian Institute on Public Affairs, which ran the Couchiching Conference? He wasn't sure. Anyway, what was going on here? Love making instead of drinking? Could it be, András asked, that for every world crisis under discussion there were three adulteries?

Two speakers on Thursday evening, Mr. Justice Chan Htoon, former attorney general of Burma and eminent Buddhist scholar, and Dr. Nasrollah Fatemi, who used to be an Iranian diplomat and who was now a professor of social science at the Farleigh Dickinson University in Teaneck, New Jersey, gave us a lot to worry about. The Burmese judge said that in Southeast Asia the communists were winning the propaganda battle hands down because they had an easy answer to every question. The progress Moscow was making in the Asian subcontinent was not clearly understood in the West, he said. "If Nehru fails in his bid to establish firmly a secular state with parliamentary institutions," he pointed out, "then the whole of the Asiatic East will fall to the Communists."

The Iranian speaker, too, pleaded for a greater understanding by the West of the situation in his part of the world. "We people of Asia," he declared, "have given the world the Ten Commandments, the Sermon of the Mount, and the religions of Islam and Buddhism, and without these, what would the western world have been?"

At the breakfast table on Friday morning, at which András sat opposite me, Claire Gorringe, an elderly lady-psychologist, said how clever that attractive Iranian speaker had been to ask that rhetorical question. She had never thought of Palestine being in Asia, she confessed.

"Asia Minor," András corrected her. "The Turks also live in Asia Minor. They sat in Hungary for centuries." He seemed to be in high spirits. Last night, I decided, he must have allowed an older woman to seduce him. "They wanted to turn Hungary into a part of Asia Minor. But we wouldn't let them."

"Good for you." Claire Gorringe patted his hand maternally and then poured maple syrup on her porridge. "The Greeks threw them out, too, as I seem to remember. The Greeks and the Jews, these were the people who made us what we are today."

"Not the Hungarians?" András asked.

Everybody, including András, laughed.

At the last session on Friday evening, the question was whether Canada could affect western strategies. Four journalists spoke under the chairmanship of the historian William Kilbourn, of McMaster University. I was there but András skipped the session.

On the three-hour train journey from nearby Longford to Union Station in Toronto, András told me what happened to him on his last night. He told me that on Thursday evening he met a beautiful divorced schoolteacher who had two married children and was expecting her first grandchild. On Friday they were to meet again, in her cabin near the tennis courts. She would be alone.

On the way to her, András told me, he passed Ann's cabin. It was dark.

She was sitting on her doorstep. He told her he was going to meet somebody.

She did not appear to find this very amusing.

In fact, András said, Ann sounded distinctly resentful. She told him that she was stuck there all alone, while her sons slept and her husband was off playing bridge somewhere. She invited him to sit with her, so she would not have to count the stars by herself.

He paused for a few seconds, then he quoted her literally: "I don't invite men further than my doorstep. So don't you get any ideas."

He said he turned to go. But she wouldn't let him. She held out her hand so he took it and helped her up. As soon as she was on her feet she pulled him towards her. They kissed—it was a long kiss, which ended suddenly when she pulled herself away to remind him—she called him *Andy*, which nobody had done before—that she had never before been unfaithful to her husband.

"Well," he responded quickly, "then don't start now."

He turned around but she drew him back.

They lay down on the grass behind the cottage.

"I had hardly started to...I don't know the right word in English—well, we had hardly..."

"Embraced," I helped him.

"Oh yes, thank you. We had hardly embraced when we heard her husband's voice in the distance. I wanted to continue since he couldn't possibly see us. But she pulled herself away and called out, 'I'm coming, dear. I just went for a walk.'"

András ran away and made his way to his original destination, hoping that his schoolteacher was still alone, waiting for him in her cottage. But as he approached he heard voices. So he did not even bother to knock at the door.

We were approaching Toronto when András told me the end of his story.

This morning, he reported, Ann was waiting for him before breakfast.

"I must talk to you," she said. "I feel so guilty."

"What on earth for?" he asked.

"What we did was wrong."

"Nonsense," he said. "We didn't really make love. We'd hardly got started when your husband called."

Ann brightened up immediately.

"You're quite right, Andy. It isn't as though we got to the point of anything serious."

"That was the first time," András said as we arrived in Union Station, "that I—what was the word you used?—oh yes, that I *embraced* a woman after which she decided I hadn't and was happy about it."

•   •   •

My thanks are due to my friend Stephen Vizenczey for giving me permission to borrow freely from his book In Praise of Older Women *(Totem Press, 1978).*

Waiting for René Lévesque

I DON'T KNOW WHY I didn't mind that every time I had dinner with Camille all she wanted to talk about was René Lévesque. I must have thought that was the price I had to pay for the considerable pleasure of her company. It was worth it: René was a remarkable character, particularly at the time of the Montreal TV producers' strike of 1958/59, which is the subject of this story.

René's marriage, his kids and his many other girlfriends did not matter to Camille. She had to put up with them or not see him at all. Or, rather, see him only on television. They had had a brief affair while they were law students at the University of Laval in Quebec City. He was late for every date and she seems to have spent most of her time waiting for him. But when they did meet, she had a marvellous time with him. He cut most of his lectures—she didn't—and he nearly flunked. He preferred to play cards, go to the movies and talk, talk, talk about serious things, among them about the uselessness of high-minded idealism unless it was linked to concrete action. That had been a theme for him all along, she said. He read every newspaper and book that caught his attention. Before Laval, he had always been an A student, she said, in New Carlisle in the Gaspé peninsula where he grew up, and then later, in

1936, after his father's death when René was fourteen, at the Jesuit college in Quebec City. He was seventeen when the war broke out.

At dinner just after Christmas, this time at Chez Ernest, once the *fondants de poisson au beurre de citron* were served, I asked Camille what René did during the war.

"He would certainly do all he could to avoid being drafted in the Canadian Army, that's for sure," she said. "And that, after 1943, became a distinct possibility. Especially if he failed his law course. You know about us French Canadians and conscription. He would do anything to avoid putting on the king's uniform."

I was in no need of a lecture on that topic.

"Let me try to imagine him," I mused, "in Quebec City in 1943, listening to the war news on the radio, from North Africa, from Russia, reports about the bombing of Germany. Would he not want to get involved in some way? Or did he hate the English more than the Nazis?"

"If he did," she said, "I was not aware of it. As far as I can remember, he had no hatred of the English at all. But how could I tell? I could never figure out what went on deep inside him. I was constantly surprised. Occasionally he even had a good word for Duplessis. [Maurice Duplessis (1890–1959) was the autocratic premier of Quebec.] But not very often. He grew up in New Carlisle – a peaceful small town on the Baie de Chaleur, just north of New Brunswick. It was English. His father was a lawyer who worked in an English-speaking firm. English was the language of the street just as much as French."

"So?"

"Instead of joining the Canadian Army, René went to New York and got a job at the United States Office of

War Information. That was early in 1944. They liked him immediately. He was bilingual and had a lot of radio experience. Radio was his element. He had started at thirteen, when he was helping out at the local station as a translator. One day the announcer fell ill, so he went on the air instead. Radio was in his blood. And in Quebec City, in 1942, while he was at Laval, he worked for station CBV, which happens to be on the French network of the CBC, of Radio Canada. The people in New York were impressed and sent him to London right away. There he worked in the studios of the OWI, broadcasting in French to Belgium and northern France. He liked London, especially Hyde Park Corner."

"And, if I may ask, did he write to you from London?"

"You may ask." She smiled. "He did. Not too often, I admit. His mother also complained about his long silences. But we got over it. Shall I go on?"

"Please do. Take your time."

"I'll try not to make it sound too boring. A year after the invasion of Europe, René was sent to the continent to report on the advance of American forces and act as liaison officer between American and French officers. In the spring of 1945, he became senior correspondent to the U.S. Seventh Army. He was with the Americans when they liberated Dachau. He would never forget it. He was getting ready for an assignment in the Pacific when they dropped that bomb on Japan. Which ended that war. So in 1946 he was back in Montreal and, very soon, he went to work for Radio Canada."

All this Camille told me while we were finishing our main courses at Chez Ernest. It was Christmas time, time to eat well. What will she have for dessert? *Fromage? Baba au rhum? Crème caramel? Profiteroles? Pâtisserie?* She chose first a piece of Rocquefort, to be followed by a *tarte aux fraises* and coffee.

"Radio Canada's International Service this time," she continued. "Not the stations in Quebec City or Montreal. He was going to broadcast to Europe. Exactly what he wanted to do. Before the war he had only read about other countries in books. The war experience had opened his eyes. He also became interested in American politics. Soon, the domestic service also used him. He covered at least one of the American political conventions. In 1951 Radio Canada sent him to Korea to report on the war, and in 1953 to London to cover the Queen's coronation. It was these assignments that made it possible for him to develop his skill in putting across, with amazing ease, complex subjects and making them seem simple and intelligible. It was this skill, that later, through *Point de Mire,* turned him into a television celebrity—no, more than that—turned him into a pioneer of serious television in Quebec. He did this as an internationalist, covering international affairs, getting everybody interested in the world outside Quebec."

René's television career happened to coincide with the spectacular rise of television. TV had started in 1952 and changed the way Quebecers thought about themselves, their province and the world at large.

"We had been isolated by our language and culture," said Camille. "Television tore off our blinkers. Especially Radio Canada. And René played a leading role in making us see the world outside. He helped us think for ourselves. And he helped us understand, among so many other things, that Duplessis was a leftover from yesterday's world."

"What does your father have to say about these things?"

Camille had told me about her father, who owned a number of houses in central Montreal, and also had a few race horses at Blue Bonnets. She was very close to him and helped him administer his properties. Camille lived with her parents in Outremont.

"Papa sits on the fence. His mind is elsewhere. He thinks I'm an idiot to waste my time on René."

However much I would have preferred Camille to pay more attention to me, I could not really agree with him.

"When am I going to meet René?" I asked in the taxi on the way home.

"I will try to arrange something for the weekend. I'll call you tomorrow evening."

She did.

"There's a serious complication," she reported. "I had to do the rounds in the apartments this morning. Some of our tenants are Radio Canada producers. The studios are close by, you know, in the old Ford Hotel, at the corner of Dorchester West and Bishop. So I talked to them. All I heard was trouble with management. They want to form a union and management won't let them. They've tried three times. The answer is always no. They're seething."

Next day, at lunch at Aux Délices, we talked about nothing else.

"Why won't management let the producers form a union?" I asked.

"Because they say producers are part of management," she explained. "Producers have budgets. They spend money on actors, writers, musicians. They're not labour, management says. They should be satisfied with having an association, they say. Which they have now. But a union that negotiates collective agreements is absolutely out of the question, management says. The law does not allow for such a thing. This attitude, of course, runs directly counter to the union movement, which, as you know, has become more and more powerful during the last few years. You've heard about the Asbestos Strike in 1949?"

I had. A nasty, violent, bitter strike that rallied the entire Quebec intelligentsia to the side of labour. And similarly, the miners' strike at Noranda.

"Doesn't management have a point?" I asked, as I helped myself to a sizeable portion of Aux Délices' famous *profiteroles.*

"Not if you listen to the producers. During the last few years they've become acutely unhappy about their working conditions, and above all with the intolerably contemptuous way their boss, André Ouimet, talks to them. After all, it's they, the producers, who created the programs that have galvanized the province, and men like Ouimet are only bureaucrats whose job it is to enable the producers to do their work. He is an example of the worst kind of old-fashioned paternalism, they say. He's their red rag. André, you know, happens to be the much younger brother of Radio Canada's president, Alphonse Ouimet. But Alphonse has had nothing to do with André's rise to power and hardly knows him. The whole thing has become very ugly. There are only seventy-four producers. But if the seven existing unions—the stagehands, the journalists, the technical people and so on—side with them they can paralyze the entire service."

"So you don't think René is in the mood to meet me?" I asked.

"I didn't say that. This thing is sheer torture for him. Everybody wants him to make a statement backing the producers. He's a big name. Many of them are his friends. He hasn't done that."

"Why not?"

"He doesn't answer me when I ask him."

There was an almost unanimous vote the day before Christmas Eve, on December 23, authorizing a strike to be called "at the opportune moment." In the days following, nobody would, or could, speak to the rebels in the Corporation's name. On the 29th they assembled in the lobby of the Radio Canada Building. It was very cold. Their leader, Fernand Quirion, publicly announced the immediate implementation of the strike vote. The actors' union announced its members would not cross the picket line. The president, Alphonse Ouimet, was summoned home from his holidays in Florida. He arrived on New Year's Day. The next day, Jean Marchand arrived in Montreal, the Secretary General of the Confédération des travailleurs catholiques du Canada, who assumed leadership of the strike. He was tough and experienced and very popular. Camille knew he was an old friend of René's. They used to play poker together at Laval when they were students. On the following days Alphonse Ouimet spoke with Fernand Quirion and others. No progress was made. This was followed by formal meetings. Again, no progress was made. Supervisory personnel kept the network on the air, mainly with news and movies.

At last, René could spare ten minutes to have a cup of coffee with us, in a greasy spoon on St. Catherine's Street west of Guy Street, where nobody would recognize him. It was still very cold. We had been waiting for him for forty-five minutes. When he came in he had the same crumpled look he did on television. He looked pale and harassed. Camille introduced me. He was perfectly polite and gave me one of his quick smiles that I already knew from watching him on the screen. I forgave him for not being in the least interested in me.

"You're mad at me for not being on the picket line," he said to Camille. "Right?"

"Right. I can't make you out at all, René."

"I'm not a producer. I'm a freelancer."

"Others in your position have joined them," Camille said. "I can rattle off the names. André Laurendeau, Gratien Gélinas, Félix Leclair, Denise Pelletier, Roger Lemelin, Pierre Trudeau, Monique Leyrac, dozens of others. Everybody's asking about you. You have backed all the other strikers on *Point de Mire* over the years. And now you're silent."

"I know, I know." He was getting angry. "You know perfectly well which side I'm on. Everybody knows. But it's not as simple as you people seem to think. I have signed a personal contract with the Corporation. I have to honour my signature."

"Okay, okay." Camille was unconvinced. "But surely, under these circumstances..."

"Yes," he suddenly shouted at her. "*Especially* under these circumstances! Radio Canada is not some sort of medieval capitalist slave driver. It's been ahead of everybody else. Where would this province be without it? And where would I be without it? I owe everything to the Corporation. Let's wait and see. Maybe there's a role I can play. But not yet."

On January 9, Fernand Quirion and Jean Marchand sent a telegram to Michael Starr, the Minister of Labour in Ottawa, requesting his intervention and a meeting with

Prime Minister John Diefenbaker, who had consistently maintained a hands-off policy.

On January 15, a new parliamentary session opened in Ottawa. The strike was immediately a subject of debate. Three days later, Alphonse Ouimet suffered a heart attack. The Executive Vice President, Ernest Bushnell, took over. "Bush," as everybody called him, was known as a thoroughly decent, genial character from Toronto whom everybody liked. In the early twenties he had sung tenor in a quartet on the Chautauqua circuit and owed his rise to power to his skill as a programmer, not to his prowess as a negotiator with alien militants.

There was only one thing that was wrong with him. He spoke no French.

On January 22 he gave notice, which he later withdrew, that all employees not at work were presumed to have resigned unless they returned within twenty-four hours.

The French press, led by *Le Devoir,* backed the producers wholeheartedly. At the University of Montreal forty professors, including two deans, demanded a resumption of negotiations and a royal commission. The producers' association in Toronto, however, made no move to support their colleagues. There was practically no communication between the two associations. The Toronto producers had no wish to form a union, in their mind an activity reserved for the working class. They had no sympathy for producers who did. As *La Presse* pointed out, the Montreal producers called the Toronto association a *club de pêche,* a fishing club.

By now the producers had formed a picket line. The weather was getting even colder. Even the donated bottles of cognac, which passed from one person to the other, failed to warm them up. Nor did the encouraging words from law professor Pierre Elliott Trudeau, who had recently broken his foot skiing in the Laurentians and had to come by taxi.

After the strike had lasted about a month, it was René's friend Jean Marchand who at last managed to persuade him to change his position—very slightly at first. Marchand had experience with strikes and was beginning to fear that the strikers' solidarity might crumble. He had to think of ways to keep their spirits up. So he managed to talk René into coming along on a march to Ottawa by train on January 27—fifteen hundred people in sixteen specially reserved CN cars—to demonstrate on Parliament Hill in the morning and to have a delegation see Michael Starr, the Labour Minister, in the afternoon.

Camille wanted to go along but she told me she did not want to embarrass René with her presence. So she thought of a ploy. One of Starr's aides owned two horses that were being cared for by her father at Blue Bonnets. One of them was to run in a race the next Sunday. This gave her a perfect opportunity to go along, on the pretext that she wished to discuss the horse's chances with the owner. As it happened, there was no need for such a ploy. René was pleased to see her on the train and did not even mind at all that she went along with the delegation to the minister's office.

There she witnessed the psychological push René received, which everybody had been waiting for.

She described the scene to me in detail the next day after they had all returned to Montreal.

In the morning there was high oratory on freezing Parliament Hill. Jean Duceppe, the head of the actors' union, called the local management in Montreal a bunch of imbeciles. He also had more colourful words for them.

They were prepared to destroy what the producers had built up, he said. In the afternoon the delegation made its way to the Ministry of Labour.

Michael Starr, the strongly anti-Soviet son of an immigrant, was the first Ukrainian to be elected mayor of a major Canadian city, Oshawa, in 1949. Three years later he won a seat in the House of Commons as a Progressive Conservative and in 1956 he had supported Diefenbaker's bid for the leadership. The labour portfolio was his reward.

Camille told me Marchand and Quirion spoke to Starr in French. He seemed to listen attentively but did not understand a word. He said he was sorry, but he did not speak French. So he spoke to them in English, which of course they all understood. He asked them to have patience. As long as the parties talked to each other, he said, there was hope for a speedy settlement.

It was René who asked him whether he knew what he was saying, whether he understood what the strike was about. Starr had to confess that he knew nothing about it and made it clear that Mr. Diefenbaker was not interested in it either. It seemed to be perfectly clear that, as far as they were concerned, Canada could happily do without French television.

Of course everybody was appalled, Camille said. Everybody *except René* saw this as the kind of thing to be expected from governments, which, after all, were always on the side of management, whatever the issue. They were used to this kind of thing from the days of Duplessis.

But for René this was categorically different. He had an eye-opening experience in that office. Only René did, nobody else. Not Marchand, not Quirion, not Duceppe, not anyone. Only he saw it as a straightforward French–English issue. It was not primarily a labour–management issue at all. It was a French–English issue. English Canada could not care less about French Canada. That is what René found.

Up to now, Camille explained to me, Quebec nationalism had been seen by one and all as primarily the property of the Union Nationale, Duplessis's party. No longer, René decided in that office. It had to become something quite different, much bigger and deeper. Quebec had to wake up to the simple truth that English Canada was behaving the way it had always behaved. The nationalism needed now had to be inspired by the sort of people who were leading this strike, by enthusiastic young people with ideas. For Michael Starr, Ukraine mattered, not Quebec. Little petty autocrats like André Ouimet were entirely the wrong target; they were of no consequence, of no interest at all. If the strike had happened in Toronto it would have lasted no longer than half an hour. No wonder the Toronto producers did not make a move. French Canada was of no interest to them. No wonder the English-speaking unions were advising their members to go back to work. No wonder the English staff producers and announcers at CBM and CBMT crossed the picket line.

Camille had said René had an eye-opening experience in Michael Starr's office. She did not say—because she could not have known—that it was in fact an epiphany that, after a long waiting period, launched him on his historic career and culminated in his role as patron saint of Quebec separatism and its first separatist premier.

Camille remained friends with him until he died in 1987.

The Canadian Broadcasting Corporation caved in. The producers won on March 7, 1959, after sixty-eight days in the cold, with a settlement that provided that their union was not to join Jean Marchand's CTCC.

At that time the Radio Canada building was on Dorchester Street, now Boulevard René Lévesque.

The Innocence of John Diefenbaker

THIS IS A WHO-DONE-IT that starts with a careless remark I made on Dominion Day—July 1, 1959—at a dinner party. The venue was the comfortable grey-stone house of Bob and Doris O'Neill in the posh Ottawa enclave of Rockcliffe, not far from Prime Minister John Diefenbaker's residence on Sussex Drive, or from Rideau Hall, the Governor General's mansion. Bob was an economist high up in the Department of Finance and Doris one of the more enterprising, political hostesses in Ottawa. The word "political" may be superfluous in this context because everything in Ottawa was political, especially after the sensational election of that flamboyant Red Tory from the West in 1957, which ended twenty-two years of Liberal rule and was followed by a landslide victory last year.

The O'Neills had been friends of mine since our days as students of political economy at the University of Toronto after the war. Bob had inherited the house from his father, who had been president of the Liberal Party. That evening they had invited a few people whose names I cannot remember, except for Rudy and Dorothy Duffy, whom I knew well. The guest of honour was Joe Westerley, a boisterous, moon-faced oil multimillionaire from Houston. He did not at all fit into the usually restrained atmosphere of a Rockcliffe dinner party, and had at least three times as many scotches before dinner as the rest of us. Westerley was in Ottawa to discuss a business project with Bob and other important people. It had nothing to do with this story.

Dominion Day happened to be the day after a special parliamentary committee cross-examined the main players in a drama that had just concluded. It was, at first, of no interest at all to Joe Westerley, but of absorbing interest to everybody else.

The hearings had made headlines across the country for an entire week. They touched on the suspicion that our prime minister had interfered with the Canadian Broadcasting Corporation, a publicly owned independent Crown corporation not run by the government but supposed to have an arm's-length relation to it. If the prime minister had interfered, he would have been guilty of an inexcusable, illegal abuse of power. Diefenbaker was a lawyer and had a life-long, seemingly genuine and much-acclaimed devotion to the law and to civil liberties that nobody, not even his Liberal foes, questioned. He had gone on record to declare that while he was prime minister there would be no interference with the CBC, by him or by any member of his government.

It was one thing making a pious declaration in cold blood, but quite another to act according to it during one of his frequent tantrums.

The high drama in the parliamentary committee had to do with—of all things—broadcasting, not exactly a bread-and-butter issue. No wonder the Texan oil tycoon was stumped. The concept of a taxpayer-supported broadcasting organization was totally alien to him. Moreover, the drama had to do with old-fashioned radio, not with the far more topical new medium of television.

A week earlier, on June 23, thirty-two producers of the CBC from all over English Canada had resigned on a matter of principle, namely the independence of the Corporation from government interference. They were acting in protest against the sudden cancellation of a daily three-and-a-half-minute radio program called *Preview Commentary,* scheduled on weekday mornings after the eight o'clock news.

Diefenbaker had never concealed his conviction that the CBC had a Liberal bias, if not actually a socialist bias. Could it be that in some way he was behind the cancellation? Or could it be that Ernie Bushnell, the amiable acting president and general manager of the Corporation, had ordered the cancellation to please him, perhaps to prevent interference? In which case it was "Bush" who had committed a grave impropriety.

If the thirty-two protesters had been members of a union, they would have gone out on strike. But, as they repeatedly indicated to the press, resigning from their jobs, after having failed in their exhaustive attempts to obtain a satisfactory explanation from their bosses for the cancellation, was their weapon of last resort. While the papers could not get enough of this—in midsummer there was not much news—resigning from the Corporation in protest was a matter of the utmost seriousness to the producers involved, many of whom had wives, husbands, mothers-in-law, children and mortgages.

"I'll tell you what I'll do tomorrow morning," Joe Westerley said. "I will phone my friend Jack Paar and have him put your prime minister with the funny name on his show, together with the CBC boss and a couple of those rebels. They'll all be friends in no time and everything will be hunky-dory."

"Excellent idea," I said among the general merriment.

"Now I wish somebody would explain to me," Joe continued happily, "why everybody is getting so excited about a little program that doesn't even have a sponsor."

Our host's explanation did not seem to satisfy him entirely.

"You know something? The way you people throw dirt at your prime minister reminds me of what we used to do to Huey Long."

Huey Long was the radical, bombastic and immensely popular governor of Louisiana in the 'thirties who, after having been accused of dictatorial tendencies, was assassinated at the height of his fame in 1935 at the State Capitol in Baton Rouge. In 1933, Huey Long had split with Roosevelt and was planning to run for president himself. His rise to power had parallels with that of Hitler in Germany.

"How fascinating that you should say that, Joe," Doris O'Neill said. She seemed to mean it, even though no doubt she also wanted to flatter her husband's wealthy visitor. "I've never thought of Dief that way. But now that you mention it...Mind you, during the Depression we had our own problems and didn't pay much attention to Louisiana."

I mentioned that among the dinner guests were Rudy and Dorothy Duffy. Rudy was a high-level accountant in the Auditor General's office, notorious for bickering with his wife at every dinner party to which they were invited.

"I think Mr. Westerley hit the nail on the head," Dorothy Duffy observed. "That's exactly what all this fuss is about—our fear that Dief will become excessively autocratic, almost like—"

Her husband did not allow her to finish the sentence.

"But darling, forgive me, that is utter nonsense," Rudy said, patting her hand. "I've never heard anybody suggest such a thing."

"Well then, Rudy, let this be the first time," his wife shot back, withdrawing her hand, stung by his patronizing tone. "Dief loves power. Power for its own sake. You can see it in his eyes when he looks at you, hoping you will never forget the moment as long as you live."

"I can testify to that," one of the guests said. "He thinks he's the messiah. Somebody said the other day that Dief suffers from clinical paranoia, like other messianic figures."

"I wouldn't be at all surprised," Dorothy Duffy said. "Whatever the diagnosis, he relishes every moment of power. He thinks he has an Appointment with Destiny. He is on top of the world. He's been the darling of the press. I mean, Rudy, wouldn't you feel larger than life if you were a theatrical firebrand from the Bible Belt with a sacred mission and the biggest majority in the House anybody ever had? Wouldn't you phone publishers all over the country and have them fire reporters who had dared to criticize you?"

"Don't answer that, Rudy," Doris O'Neill said among general laughter.

"And Dief was sixty-two when he at last made it," Dorothy Duffy continued, unperturbed. "He never had any ambition other than to become prime minister. Remember, he first ran for a seat in 1925. It took him—let me see—twenty-seven years and I don't know how many defeats. At every level. He never gave up. Grim determination won out at last. Can you imagine what it did to him last year when Lady Churchill took him aside and whispered to him that Winston was so pleased by his election *that he danced?* At his age! That happened when Dief was in London for the Commonwealth Conference. The Churchills had him over to dinner at their place in Hyde Park Gate. Dief told everybody about it afterwards. And Winston had said, in front of everybody, that his election was the most important event in the entire world since the end of the war. Wouldn't that turn your head?"

Rudy thought it was below his dignity to answer his wife's question.

"I certainly wouldn't go around telling the CBC how to behave," he mumbled. "Especially after having accused the Liberals many times of trying to do the very same thing. Remember Dief's sarcasm, as leader of the opposition two years ago, when he asked Louis St. Laurent whether he found it possible to 'bifurcate' himself between being prime minister and an ordinary citizen? St. Laurent did nothing worse than write a letter to the chairman of the CBC's board criticizing two little talks by a university professor because he didn't like the tone of persiflage the professor used. These were his very words. Dief even wanted him to produce the letter, to see whether it was written on official stationary. Anyway, the rule that prime ministers must keep their fingers off the CBC has nothing to do with any fear of a Hitler. The model is the revered mother of the CBC—the BBC—which has the same rule. It dates back to the early 'twenties, long before any dictator was in the picture."

Joe Westerley shook his head.

"All this is beyond me," he groaned. "What you people should worry about is that some lunatic sponsor may want to interfere. After all, he who pays the fiddler calls the tune."

This was the cue for our host to give his guest a lecture about the way we Canadians do things. We didn't have state broadcasting, Bob O'Neill explained, like Radio Moscow. No minister runs the CBC. The CBC reports to Parliament through a minister, at the moment George Nowlan, the Minister of National Revenue, who had to answer questions about its conduct but had no authority whatsoever to run it.

Joe Westerley found this totally unconvincing, nor could he accept that any civilized country would allow its government to pay a single cent for broadcasting unless it wanted to sponsor a program.

"Who's in charge of the CBC at the moment?" he asked.

"The president is ill," Bob O'Neill replied. "Therefore, it's the executive vice-president, who's also general manager. He's temporarily in charge. His name is Ernie Bushnell. I know him well. A very nice man."

"Jack the Ripper was also a very nice man." Doris O'Neill observed. She was not known as a great wit for nothing. "A charming raconteur, everybody said."

After we had all agreed that killing people was usually wrong, and that good and bad behaviour were contingent, at least to some extent, on circumstances, her husband, Bob O'Neill, repeated that he knew Bush was a thoroughly decent, genial man whom everybody liked, a great programmer who loved the CBC passionately. "There was no other radio as yet, Joe," he said.

"Tell me again, please," Joe Westerley said. "Of what particular crime did the rebels accuse him?"

"A lot of people and even some newspapers call them freedom fighters, not rebels," Bob corrected him. "They accuse him of cancelling *Preview Commentary* for a reason that even their immediate superior, a man generally known as Bud Walker, said was done because of political influence from outside the Corporation."

"Please remind me, what again was that program?"

"Little political opinion pieces after the morning news from reputable Ottawa journalists on what was going on in the nation's capital. Sometimes, naturally, they were critical of the government. At other times they praised it. Sometimes they did both. The journalists were chosen with the greatest care."

"Now tell me the truth," Joe Westerley said. "Why do you think that man—what was his name?—cancelled the program?"

"Ernie Bushnell. Bush says he did nothing of the sort. He says he had always thought of the show as merely experimental. All he had done was to order the substitution of impersonal news reports instead. He thought the Ottawa journalists didn't have enough time to give their subjects the sufficiently mature thought required to form solid opinions and therefore that these talks simply weren't good enough."

"Do the rebels dispute his right to cancel the program if that is what he thought?" the tycoon asked.

"No, Joe. Everybody agrees management has the right to manage. But there are certain procedures that management must follow. It can't just give peremptory orders, without explanation and discussion. Bush did not follow these procedures."

"Did he say his action was based only on his own judgement," Joe Westerley asked, "or that he had received complaints from anybody?"

"He said some businessmen and schoolteachers had told him they didn't like a few of the talks. But at the parliamentary hearing he emphasized that he had not received any instructions from anybody in power and had not yielded to any pressure from anybody. And of one thing I am sure—Bush is not a liar."

That is when I made my historic move.

"Well," I said, without thinking about it for more than a second, "I think one should pursue this matter and find out why he acted the way he did."

"All right, my friend," Bob O'Neill retorted, pointing a finger at me. *"You* go ahead and find out."

"I will, I will."

So, suddenly, I was a sleuth. But I didn't mind. Full of energy and self-confidence, I cheerfully went to work to find out what happened. Ernie Bushnell's past as the tenor in a barbershop quartet in the 'twenties was unlikely to throw much light on the matter. Unfortunately I was not in a position to subpoena any of the CBC executives involved. Why would they talk to me? The producers, of course, would tell me their tales of woe with the greatest pleasure.

But first I contacted a few musicians who had nothing to do with *Preview Commentary*. I knew that musicians were talented gossips. I went to Toronto and questioned three members of the CBC Orchestra—a violinist, a bassoonist and a trumpeter. They met my objectives perfectly. We met in the CBC cafeteria on Jarvis Street.

They knew nothing specific about the affair but had been told that Bush was exhausted and severely overburdened, having had a rotten six months since the president fell ill. The year had begun with a similar affair, they reminded me—the producers' strike in Montreal, also on a matter of principle, but another principle, the right to form a union. It was a far more bitter dispute than this one, with important political overtones and possible consequences, and had lasted for sixty-eight days, many of which the strikers had spent picketing in the Arctic cold.

Bush had once declared publicly that "The only time I worry is when I mix scotch with rye." It must be assumed that his inability to deal with the French producers in their own language and his desperate struggle to grasp the issues involved had driven him to consume more scotch with rye than usual. This recent little gentlemanly *démarche* about a simple black-and-white issue—did he or didn't he cancel *Preview Commentary*—was over after a mere six days. But it had involved Bush personally in a sense that the other one had not. It had also involved the CBC board. When the producers resigned, the board held an emergency session and accepted the resignations. There was a huge uproar in the press. The board met again and reversed itself, thereby enabling everybody to go back to work.

All this put Bush in a most uncomfortable position. The producers, on the other hand, had won the everlasting admiration of freedom lovers all over the country, which was ample compensation for the loss of a week's pay.

"Don't forget Marguerite d'Youville," the violinist said with a leering grin. It was not immediately clear to me why the bassoonist winked and the trumpeter smirked. But then I remembered that musicians are not only great gossips but also lovers of racy stories. I don't know of any exceptions.

"Poor Bush had to deal with that, too. You see, many of the people in the French network are lapsed Catholics. They put on a play about Marie-Marguerite, the founder of the Grey Nuns, in which the heroine, before she became a nun, bounced voluptuously on a double bed with her lover in a low-cut nightgown. This was just one of many scenes that were meant to shock. So Bush had to deal with the incensed Roman Catholic hierarchy. And both his parents had been devout Methodists."

"And what about Joyce Davidson?" the trumpeter asked. "How can you ignore her?"

"Oh, I am so sorry," the violinist lamented. "How could I have overlooked Joyce. I certainly have not forgotten the row in Parliament when, just as one of our interminable royal tours began, she said—and here I quote—'Like most Canadians I am rather indifferent to the Queen's visit.' And Joyce is by far the most beautiful and popular interviewer on English television."

I recalled that hundreds of people, no doubt not all of them Empire Loyalists, had bombarded the CBC switchboards.

"Poor Bush," the trumpeter said, "had to take her off the air until the furor had died down. And he knew that she had been perfectly right. That takes a lot out of a man."

My next appointment was with Marion Johnston, whom I knew from way back. I had not seen her for some years, but I remembered her voice, a lovely, expressive, velvety contralto. She was a public affairs producer, one of those who had resigned. We met for a drink on the roof of the Park Plaza Hotel.

I gave her a tough grilling.

"Do you agree that no one was present when Dief told Bush to take it off?"

"We never said something that crude actually happened. In fact, that's the whole point."

"I suggest that you are imagining things. You imagine people behaved in a way you wanted them to behave so that you could scream bloody murder afterwards."

"Bullshit!" She was getting angry. "Our boss, Frank Peers, was told by his superior, Bud Walker, that there is no explanation for the cancellation other than political pressure. Walker told this also to the parliamentary committee hearing. Parliament accepted it. Why can't you? What more do you want?"

"I submit to you," I replied in a tone I had learned from courtroom scenes in the movies, "that your boss accepted it because he wanted to accept it. I will go further and submit to you also that he thought Dief was exactly the type who would exert pressure and Bush was exactly the type who would yield to it. Both fitted his preconceptions. And yours."

"I repeat: you are talking absolute bullshit." By now Marion was furious with me. "If you knew Frank, such nonsense would never occur to you. He is coldly analytical and super, super cautious. Everybody, especially his superiors, knows this and that is why we all followed him and resigned as he had, at very real personal cost. None of us could be sure that the Corporation would take us back."

"Of course you knew! This is Canada!"

"What's wrong with you?" she shouted. People at the next table were beginning to pay attention. "Why don't you listen to me? Let me describe this man to you. Frank Peers is conscientious to a fault, almost inhumanly so, ridiculously incorruptible, scrupulously judicious, unbelievably unemotional, a little severe but not without a sense of humour, in total self-control. Nobody knows what goes on inside him. It is his responsibility to see to it that the Corporation is not swayed for a single minute from the path of independence and impartiality. Nobody takes his responsibilities more seriously."

"Well," I yielded, "one of these days you must introduce me to this paragon of virtue. The fact remains it's his word against Bush's. Forget all those in between. Bush testified that he acted because he and others thought the program was bad and for no other reason. Did Parliament say to him 'We don't believe you'?"

"No. Everybody shrugged and left it at that."

"Why? Isn't lying to Parliament the one unpardonable sin? Why didn't they go after him? Why did they let him off the hook?"

"That's easy," Marion replied. "If they had found Bush guilty of lying and decided that in fact he had yielded to pressure, it would have meant that they would have to accuse this nice man of contempt—obviously they'd rather not do that. So they preferred to shrug and let it go. That was less trouble."

A new light was suddenly switched on in my brain.

"What about that minister, the man who has to answer questions about the CBC in the House but has no authority for running it? The Minister for National Revenue, if I remember right. What was his name?"

"George Nowlan. He also testified in the committee. He said he didn't do it."

"He's a lawyer, isn't he?"

"I believe so. From Nova Scotia."

"Well, Marion," I said after a few seconds' quiet meditation, "I think I should look at him a little more closely. Don't you?"

"Go right ahead," she said, obviously convinced that this would lead me nowhere. "And let me know what happens."

The next morning I went back to Ottawa. My father is a member of the Rideau Club. I knew the barman, an elderly Scotsman with a little white mustache who looked more distinguished than most of his customers. The barman knew and liked me. He was, of course, in a unique position to know everything that was going on.

I ordered a scotch and soda and told him about my mission. I wondered if he had followed the hearings of the parliamentary committee.

"Oh yes," he laughed. "The heads-will-roll hearings."

I looked puzzled.

"You haven't heard? In that case you haven't paid attention. The phrase came up at the hearings. Repeatedly."

"I'm sorry I must have missed it. In what connection?"

"When Bush was in Toronto, he and Bud Walker went to the Celebrity Club for a drink. You know, that place opposite the CBC building. It was a little more than a week ago, the same day as those resignations. They went to the back to telephone the CBC president at home and tell him what was going on. The poor, sick man had not heard a thing about it. Bush did the talking. He told the president, in Walker's presence, that the president's head, his own head and maybe also the minister's head would roll if they didn't pull up their socks, whatever that meant. This can't have speeded up the president's convalescence, can it? Bush later confirmed at the hearing that he used the phrase in that telephone conversation with the president."

"You mean heads would roll if they didn't cancel the program?"

"He didn't say that. He said heads would roll because of the series of rather tragic circumstances in the last six months. Those were his words. And he added that such rolling of heads would be quite proper if it was felt that the CBC was incompetently run."

"I see." I gave this a moment to sink in. "I wonder what other heads they were talking about," I said. "Probably also George Nowlan's."

"No doubt," the Scotsman laughed. "I think that is rather amusing, don't you? You must have heard that when Nowlan was asked at the hearing whether he had been told that his head might roll, he said yes he had heard that, but he wanted to know whether this was a promise or a threat! He couldn't wait for this to happen. He was thoroughly fed up with handling the CBC file, he said, in addition to his heavy duties as Minister of National Revenue."

"And was he asked whether he ever told Bush to take off *Preview Commentary*?"

"Of course. He replied he wouldn't have dreamed of doing such a dastardly thing. He often talked about CBC matters with his good friend Ernie Bushnell. Nowlan had always told him frankly what he thought about his sloppy management and his insubordinate producers, but running the CBC was Bush's affair, *he* was the general manager, not him, George Nowlan. If they wanted him to run the CBC, Nowlan said, he was not their boy. And Bush told the committee that the CBC has never had a better, more hands-off minister than George Nowlan since the very beginning."

I uttered a deep sigh.

"If Nowlan didn't do it," I said, more to myself than to the barman, "who did?"

"May I give you some constructive advice?" the barman whispered to me through a cupped hand. "Talk to Mary Stillman, Nowlan's Girl Friday. She'll tell you."

I don't want to boast, but I cannot conceal my pride at the way I solved the almost insoluble tactical and strategic obstacles that stood in my way to Mary Stillman's confidence. It took me only a day to establish that she was one of the toughest and most powerful executive assistants in Ottawa, that her loyalty to the minister was bulletproof, that she was the soul of discretion, that no one got to see the minister without her permission, that she was in total control of his schedule, his telephone and his correspondence. I also discovered that everybody, including Dief himself—not to mention Mrs. Nowlan—was a little afraid of her, though it had to be added that Dief liked her immensely and had once even tried to snatch her from his old friend. When Mary laughingly told her boss about this, Nowlan phoned Dief immediately and told him he would join the Liberals the moment he tried it again.

How did I find her?

I am not going to say I was lucky. I worked hard to discover the way, eliminating dozens of possible but ultimately unpromising avenues. Luck had nothing to do with it. I discovered that Mary had one weakness—she loved playing bridge. She did not belong to a bridge club, but every Thursday evening she played with three old friends, all colleagues now occupying middle positions in the civil service, in the home on Slater Street of one of them, Claire Hogan, an ingenious and adventurous lady who worked in the Bureau of Statistics and happened to be a friend of my mother's. (Okay, I admit *that* was a coincidence.) I told Claire the truth and asked her to invite me to stay in her guestroom. I deposited my suitcase in the afternoon when I arrived from Toronto.

At around ten thirty that evening they were playing their fourth rubber. Claire introduced me. They nodded politely and continued playing. Mary was a rather ordinary-looking, middle-aged lady, a little plump, who looked far less imposing than I had imagined. I went to my room. When they finished, Claire always gave them a cup of tea and some strawberry tarts. That was my signal to emerge. We made small talk. Claire managed to prevent Mary from leaving with the others and gave her a second cup of tea. She said I was a nephew of Ernie Bushnell's, but relations between us were temporarily strained, for some foolish family reason, adding that I had followed last week's hearings with the greatest interest and was baffled by my uncle's testimony.

"One of these days I'm going ask him directly," I told Mary. "But I can't at the moment."

"I understand," she said. "Families can be the very devil."

"I mean, all these people are saying there had been political pressure, and he is denying it. I can't make it out at all. They couldn't have invented it. They must have based it on *something*. They're all honest men who don't tell lies."

"Nobody told a lie," Mary stated categorically.

"Well," I smiled, "that's good to know. But...?"

"You don't believe me?" she asked amiably. "Let me tell you what happened. I like Bush and I think the CBC is great. All Bush said to Parliament was that there was no political pressure from anybody speaking to him officially, or purporting to speak to him officially for the government. That is perfectly true. Now listen to this. From time to time Dief drops in, usually unannounced. I try—but I can't keep him out of the office. He just glares at me with his big blue eyes, as if to say 'What's the point of being prime minister, after a lifetime of trying, if I don't have the right to barge in on my friends?' So he came in, once again, for the simple reason of having one of his tantrums and giving my minister hell for allowing the CBC to be run by a bunch of Liberals. No, worse—a bunch of socialists! He was holding him personally responsible. Every morning, on his way to work, his driver turns on that program *Preview Commentary* on the car radio. It ruins the day for him. If he, George Nowlan, didn't ask the general manager of the CBC to cancel that darned program immediately he would cut the CBC appropriations by fifteen million dollars. I knew my minister wouldn't tell Bush. So naturally I phoned him at home that very evening. Nobody has ever told me not to interfere with the CBC!"